Photoshop

The beginners guide to Photoshop, Editing Photos, Photo Editing Tips, and How to Improve your Photography with Photoshop!

Table of Contents

Introduction

I want to thank you and congratulate you for downloading the book, *"Photoshop"*.

This book contains helpful information about Photoshop, and how you can use it.

For photographers, Photoshop is a powerful tool. Whilst it is best to take as good of a picture as you can initially, things don't always look as perfect as you may want.

Oftentimes, the lighting might be off, there could be blemishes that need covering up, or maybe the framing of your photo isn't correct. With Photoshop, these can all be fixed in a matter of minutes!

This book includes great tips and techniques that will help you to improve and edit your photos with the use of Photoshop! You will learn all of the basics that any aspiring photographer should know, and be able to easily take your photography to the next level!

You will learn about the different tools and features that Photoshop has, and how to understand and use them accordingly. With a little practice, you will be confidently editing photos like a professional!

Thanks again for downloading this book, I hope you enjoy it!

Chapter 1 - Photoshop Toolbar Overview

Using Photoshop can be an intimidating task for many beginners. However, the application has many vital features that can benefit many novice photographers and graphic artists in particular; therefore, despite the added challenge, they should learn to utilize the photo editing tool if they wish to become better at their chosen craft. If you are one of the many interested Photoshop users who have long wanted to use the application but don't know where to start, then this book will help equip you with all the Photoshop basics you need.

Where to get Photoshop?

The first thing that you will need to address before learning about any photo editing basics is actually installing the software on your PC. Unfortunately, the Adobe Photoshop software is not available for free. Nevertheless, Adobe does offer interested users the chance to try a 30-day Photoshop software trial free of charge.

While you will eventually need to purchase the software at full price at the end of the trial period, those 30 days will be enough to help you learn the basics of the software. At the end of that trial period, you should have enough working knowledge about the various Photoshop features.

The Photoshop Interface

When you first open your Photoshop software, you will notice a large toolbar located at the left side of the canvas. Some of the tools have functions that are straightforward enough that you can easily understand them from their names alone. However, other unfamiliar tools such as the lasso tool and magic wand will need a little more explanation.

Though this overview is by no means extensive or exhaustive, it will undoubtedly help you familiarize yourself with most of the tools on the Photoshop toolbar. You will be able to gather enough information regarding the individual uses of each tool so that you can immediately start using these tools to edit and play around with your photos.

The Move Tool

The Move tool has a form that is similar to a regular mouse icon. However, its function is slightly different from that of the humble mouse. Instead of allowing you to click various buttons, the Move tool does as its name implies and allows users to move objects in and around a selected layer. Simply click on any object or location on the canvas and move it to your liking.

The Marquee Tool

The Marquee tool is the perfect tool to help you select any part of the Photoshop canvas to form a specific shape. The default shapes that you can create using the Marquee tool include the rectangle and ellipse. However, by holding down that shift key, you can turn the rectangle into a square and the ellipse into a perfect circle.

The Lasso Tool

The Lasso tool is a Photoshop selection tool that enables users to create any free form shape on the canvas. The selected area will look like there is a lasso that holds it together; hence, the name.

Aside from the plain lasso, you also have the option to create a polygonal lasso or a magnetic lasso. As the name implies, the polygonal lasso creates a selection with set corners instead of creating a free form shape. The polygonal lasso allows users to set specific points on the canvas that they can link together to form their desired shape.

Meanwhile, the magnetic Lasso is particularly useful for images that already have defined edges. Instead of manually selecting your desired points, the magnetic lasso automatically detects the dividing edges between images on a layer and forms a selection.

The Magic Wand Tool

The Magic Wand tool is similar to the magnetic lasso tool in a way that it automatically selects an area on your canvas. However, as an added feature, the Magic Wand can automatically select areas that are similar to one another. It can therefore serve as an easy way of selecting the background of your image and deleting it. Unfortunately, the results using the Magic Wand to delete backgrounds are often less than satisfactory and you may end up with numerous unwanted white or black spots.

The Crop Tool

The Crop tool functions in the way that you would expect. It can crop any picture to your desired size. If you have a specific size in mind, then you are also free to input the desired proportions so that the tool can apply these to the image with a single click.

The Eyedropper Tool

The Eyedropper tool has an icon that has a similar appearance to an actual eyedropper. However, instead of acting as a remedy of sorts, the Eyedropper tool allows you to select any part of your canvas and use the detected color in any way that you please. You can use the sampled color to change your foreground, background, image color, etc. It is particularly useful for creating copies of a logo or image with a specified color scheme.

The Healing Brush Tool

As the name suggests, the Healing Brush tool fixes any imperfections on your photo. However, instead of automatically healing any spot, you will have to select a specific area on your image manually by using the alt key so that the tool can blend that selection over any similar areas. This tool is particularly useful in blurring fine lines, blemishes, sunspots and other facial imperfections in portraits.

The Clone Stamp Tool

The Clone Stamp tool has a similar function as the healing brush tool. However, instead of blurring over the areas to blend them in, the clone stamp merely stamps one selected area over another area.

The Pencil and Paintbrush Tools

The Pencil and Paintbrush tools function in the same way as their real world counterparts. However, the advantage of these virtual artist tools is that you can easily change their thickness and size at the click of a button. It is also possible to paint or draw using various shapes by simply downloading additional software.

The History Brush Tool

The History Brush tool functions like an edit and undo button in one. Though Photoshop unfortunately only records 50 changes at any given time, the history brush tool can still help you go back to a previous color or edit without the need to redo the entire canvas.

The Eraser Tool

The Eraser tool is similar to an actual eraser. The only difference is that this eraser can erase not only pencil marks, but paint and entire images and backgrounds as well.

The Paint Can and Gradient Tools

The Paint Can tool allows users to fill in a specific area with a preselected color. Though it is possible to edit the opacity and saturation manually, you can speed up the process by simply using the Gradient tool. Additionally, the gradient tool can blend in two different colors.

The Blur, Sharpen, and Smudge Tools

The Blur tool will help you blur your brushstrokes, the Sharpen tool will sharpen them, and the Smudge will smudge the edges to create a seamless finish. These three tools generally act as accompaniments to your paintbrush tool.

You can also use them individually even without using the paintbrush beforehand. The smudge tool is particularly useful in creating smoke effects on your images.

The Burn, Dodge, and Sponge Tools

Again, these three tools have similar functions as the paintbrush accompaniments in creating effects on your image. You can adjust all these tools to any desired size to cover a specific area.

Individually, the Burn tool can make any selected area darker. Conversely, the Dodge tool can lighten the area. Finally, the Sponge tool can adjust the color saturation of your desired area.

The Pen Tool

The Pen tool is one of the more complicated tools you will find on Photoshop. It is used to create vector images and as such is more often used on vector software such as Adobe Illustrator. Nevertheless, it can still prove to be a useful photo-editing tool due to its ability to create a desired path on your canvas.

The Path Tool

After creating a path using the Pen tool, the Path tool will allow you to play around with these paths. It functions in a similar way as the move tool, though it specifically caters to paths instead of general objects.

The Type Tool

The Type tool allows users to add text on your image or canvas. The default format for your text is a horizontal line. However, it is also possible to create vertically aligned texts as well as change your font style, size and color.

The Shape Tool

The Shape tool is a familiar tool that you can find on other editing software and even on Microsoft Word. Users can use it to create vector shapes such as squares, circles, and other polygonal shapes. Graphic artists can also use it to create customized shapes.

The Zoom and Hand Tools

The Zoom tool allows user to zoom in to any specific area that requires meticulous attention. In order to zoom out of the area, you will have to select the zoom out option manually.

Meanwhile, the Hand tool has a similar function to the move tool. However, it will only allow users to navigate around the canvas if they are currently zoomed in to a specific potion on the canvas.

Chapter 2 - The Layers Palette

Layers are often mentioned alongside any discussion that involves Photoshop. In many cases, layers will determine whether you will end up with a beautifully edited image or an over-processed mess. Though many novice users might be intimidated with an essentially unfamiliar tool, they will soon discover just how essential layers can be when it comes to post-processing images on Photoshop.

What are Layers?

In brief, layers will allow users to work on separate parts of the image without affecting the other sections. Opening multiple layers and adjusting them individually will help you better keep track of your edits and adjustments.

To make the layers more manageable, you can adjust their opacity to a lower percentage so that they will be barely visible. You are also free to move them around and blend them.

The easiest way to grasp the Photoshop layers concept is by thinking of them as pieces of tracing paper or acetate that can help you edit an image without directly affecting the original photo. It is also possible to edit multiple areas on a single layer. You may also designate a single area to each layer for more control. Layer masks can also enable you to blend layers together or hide specific areas.

Active and Hidden Layers

To better concentrate on any single portion of your image, Photoshop gives users the option to hide any layers that they are not actively working on. The eye icons shown at the right panel of the canvas indicate the currently active layers. Clicking on the eye will temporarily hide the layer from view without necessarily removing the applied changes.

The Blending Mode located at the upper part of the Layers Palette allows you to control the opacity levels of your selected layer. The Trash Can Icon at the bottom right of the panel deletes the selected layer. Meanwhile, the Add New Layer icon sits just beside it.

The icon composed of a small rectangle and circle indicates the Layer Mask option. Finally, to add more Adjustment Layers to your canvas, simply access the split circle icon on the right panel.

The Layers Palette will display not only the active layers, but their individual contents as well. You also have the option of manually naming each layer for better organization and management. This way, you will be able to find which layer you need to go to depending on the changes you need to make.

3 Essential Layer Tips

1. Creating multiple layers means that one layer corresponds to a given object or section on your image. To edit any given section, you will first have to select the layer on the Layers Palette manually to make it active. The changes performed on this layer will not affect any of the other layers. The currently active layer will be the one highlighted on the right panel.

2. The visibility eye icon not only hides your layer, but also disables it temporarily. If the eye icon is not present, you will not be able to initiate any changes on that layer. To work on a hidden layer, simply click on where the eye icon used to be to reactivate it.

3. You can adjust multiple layers to any desired stacking order. Dragging the layers to lower or higher positions on the Layers Palette can help you manage which layers have a higher priority or might need more editing.

Chapter 3 - Color Correcting Images

Now that you have learned about the basic functions of the Photoshop tools, you are ready to start using them on your pictures. You can now create professional looking images that have been color corrected, retouched and enhanced to perfection.

Again, what you will learn here are only the basics of the photo editing skills that you can use in Photoshop. Though the methods might not be exceedingly complex, they will nonetheless do a fine job in making your images look their best. Likewise, you will find that they will be more than enough to fix most of your image retouching issues.

Color Correcting your Images

Though color correction might seem like a task only a professional graphic artist can handle, any person with knowledge on basic color theory can easily perform the task. The basics of color theory lie on complementary colors. These colors lie on the opposite ends of the color wheel and essentially cancel each other out. The commonly used complementary color combinations are red-green, yellow-violet, and blue-orange.

Another useful color correcting skill is being able to decipher between colors in an image. This way, you will be able to notice what colors dominate your image and adjust them accordingly. For example, an image with prominent blue undertones connotes a melancholic feeling due to the cool color. You can then adjust the colors to achieve a more neutral or warmer tone.

Using the Histogram

Though a keen eye for detail can help you identify the dominating colors simply by looking at the image, the Histogram is a tool that can help take out the guesswork out of the process. You can find the Histogram tool in the Window menu via a drop down box.

Once you select the tool, you will be shown a window that is divided into three portions. The right side of the window represents the highlights on your image, the left side represents the shadows and the middle potion represents the mid-tones. Based on the percentage of the indicated colors on the Histogram, you will be able to pinpoint the single dominating color so that you can immediately initiate a suitable remedy.

Adjustment Tools

Photoshop has a number of specialized tools that you can use to address any color correcting issue. Some of these tools are useful when dealing with a single layer, while others can deal with multiple layers at a given time.

Single layer adjustment tools are commonly located in the Image menu. Simply select the Adjustments option and choose the most suitable one for your needs.

Meanwhile, to address color-correcting issues for multiple layers, you have two options. The first option is to select the adjustment from the Adjustment palette. The second option is to create a separate Adjustment layer by accessing the Layers menu before selecting a specific adjustment option.

The Color Balance Tool

The Color Balance tool is suitable for applying minor changes and adjustments as quickly as possible. Unfortunately, users cannot easily modify this tool according to their specific needs. It is best suited only for speedy color touch-ups at most.

One issue that it can quickly address is for cases when there is too much red in the photo's highlighted areas. The easiest way to fix this is by selecting the highlight's radio button and adjusting the levels to add more blue to balance out the red.

The Color Balance tool can also help create color effects in the shadows, highlights, and mid-tones of your pictures. The best way to learn about this tool's potential is to put it to use and play around with its options.

For more meticulous color correction fixes, the Curves tool will prove to be the more suitable option. It gives users more flexibility to adjust levels with more ease and effectiveness.

Using the Curves Tool

While some Photoshop beginners might feel intimidated simply by looking at the Curves window, it is undoubtedly the best color-correcting tool that you have at your disposal. It can accomplish a variety of needed image adjustments while giving you the versatility you need to maximize your results.

You will have the option to set your own points so that you can adjust either a few specific channels or the entire image at once. Making a point on your image simply means clicking on the curved line and dragging it upwards, downwards, left, or right. Pulling it towards the bottom right corner of the window will darken the image. Conversely, dragging the point towards the upper left corner will brighten the image. The middle portion of the line indicates the mid-tones of your image.

Adjusting Levels

The Levels tool is the more basic form of the Curves tool. This tool simplifies the adjustment option into three separate sliding levers. The shadows slider is located at the left and adjusts the intensity of the shadows on your image. The highlights slider, which is located on the right, is responsible for adjusting the intensity of your highlights. Finally, the mid-tones slider located in the middle will make the photo brighter or darker simply by moving the slider to the right or left. Generally, the sliders will affect the contrast levels of your photo.

To edit the brightness level of your image, you will need to access the Output Levels tool. The default application of the Output Levels tool will affect the entire image. By moving the black slider towards the white slider, you will be able to lighten the image. Conversely, by moving the white slider towards the black one, you will be able to darken your image.

If you wish to select only a specific color or area on your image, you can access the drop down menu on the Levels panel to select your desired color. Change the color space from CMYK to RGB or vice versa then select the specific color you want to brighten or darken.

Chapter 4 - Performing Photo Enhancements

The key to making photo enhancements look as seamless as possible is by exercising a certain level of restraint and subtlety. Though almost every portrait will need a few tweaks here and there to address the imperfections on the skin, you should learn to perform touch-ups effectively in order to lessen the chances of ending up with an overly edited image.

Using the Healing Brush and Clone Stamp to Perform Touch-ups

As briefly discussed in the first chapter, the healing brush and the clone stamp tool can perform a good job in fixing any minor issues. They can easily remove a blemish or two so that your portrait model will end up looking his or her best.

Portrait Enhancement

The main objective of portrait enhancement is not to make your model look unrecognizable; instead, it is to bring out the best in him or her. A photo will usually emphasize more details that people will not be able to get from a single glance. Being able to zoom into your image will increase the chances of over editing. To avoid this, set a limit for your enhancements and adjustment and instead, aim to make the portrait model look beautiful but still natural.

Adjusting Color Channels

The Color Channels tool allows you to adjust the individual colors in your image. The Color Channels palette is not located on your toolbar. Instead, you can find it on the right part of your canvas.

The most common color space you will see under the color channels palette is RGB. RGB stands for the colors red, green and blue. The combination of these three colors results in the image you see on your screen.

In order to determine the differences between colors, you will have to select each color individually. The red channel has the greatest amount of highlights. The blue channel has the greatest amount of detail. Finally, the green channel combines the highlights and details of the blue and red channels.

Manually adjusting the red color channel is particularly useful in editing colored portraits. The easiest way to make an adjustment is to select the red channel on the Color Channels palette. Afterwards, select all using the ctrl + A key on your PC or Command + A on your Mac and copy your image. Go back to your RGB channel then proceed to your Layers palette to paste the red channel. This will create a new layer on top of your original image that only displays the red channel.

Now since you do not want a solid red layer as your portrait, you will need to adjust the layer opacity. Proceed to the Layers palette once again and select Overlay as your Blending Mode. Reduce the opacity from 100% to 20% or lower depending on your needs. Adjusting the slider will have an immediate effect on your canvas so that you can easily gauge the percentage you need to achieve your desired result. This simple Color Channel correction can improve your portrait model's skin texture, contrast and significantly improve the image's overall color.

Using the Burn and Dodge Tools

As discussed in Chapter 1, the Burn and Dodge Tools add shadows and highlights respectively. In a way, these two tools function the same way as makeup brushes do. You can use them to create highlights and contour your portrait. They are suitable for editing even male portraits since the effects they create are often subtle and natural.

To use these tools effectively in image enhancements, you will have to look at your flat image as if it is a 3D model. You will have to add contrast to the areas that need contouring and definition to facial features such as the nose, mouth and eyes.

Contrast is achievable by using the Burn tool to add more shadows to the sides of the nose, inner corners of the lips and to define the eyebrows and eyelashes. Meanwhile, the Dodge tool can be used to further brighten the highlights on the lips, cheekbones and white portion of the eyes.

Though the end results of these adjustments might result in only minor enhancements, less is often more when it comes to using Photoshop. In truth, comparing the original image with the enhanced image is the best way to see just how much of an improvement those small changes in color and contrast can have on your image.

Chapter 5 - Editing Landscape Photographs

Whether you are an amateur or professional photographer, you will first need to master the basics of the art form before you start snapping those pictures. The key skills that you will need to apply in all of your images are composition, color theory and lighting. Likewise, you will need to have a keen visual eye to see details that most would take for granted.

However, sometimes, even the most meticulous photographer and the most powerful camera is still unable to capture that once in a lifetime moment as perfectly as you would want. It is in those cases that some basic post-processing knowledge would come in handy. Photoshop can help you edit your landscape photos to perfection by setting the exposure levels, cropping and fixing the contrast and saturation levels.

Choosing your Image

Before you get started on editing your image, you should first identify the main problems of your photograph. This way, you will have a clear idea of your editing tasks and the remedies that you can apply.

For many landscape photographs, the most obvious problem you will see is a visibly crooked horizon line. In your rush to capture that perfect moment, you might forget to photograph with a level horizon line. Thankfully, you can easily straighten that image out in Photoshop without affecting the quality.

Straightening an Image

To create a straight line using Photoshop, you will need to use a ruler much like you would on a piece of paper. The Ruler tool is not immediately visible on the Photoshop toolbar. You will need to find the Eyedropper tool first and hold it down with your mouse until it shows you more options.

Select the Ruler tool from these options and bring it towards the horizon line of your image. Click on one end of the horizon line and drag the Ruler tool straight across to the other end before releasing it. After affixing the tool, you will then click on the option that says "straighten" to make the horizon line more level.

Cropping an Image

Fixing the horizon line of your landscape photograph often results in an image that is skewed from the working surface. To eliminate the white spaces left on the corners and edges of the canvas, you will need to crop your main picture.

Simply access the Crop tool on the toolbox. When the crop outline appears on your image, drag the outline to your desired shape and size. The crop tool will create the new borders for your image.

If you end up cropping too much of your image, the shortcut to undo most Photoshop tasks is ctrl + Z. However, for PC users, the shortcut key can also be the three-step alt + ctrl + Z.

Adjusting Levels and Exposure

Another problem that you may often get in landscape photographs includes overly dark or overexposed areas. This issue obscures some of the details that you originally wanted to emphasize in your composition.

To adjust the contrast of your image, you will need to access the Levels tool under the Adjustments option. Move the arrows to the left or to the right side of the Levels slider to fix the contrast of your image. To lighten dark areas, move the slider to the far left. Meanwhile, to darken overexposed areas, move the slider to the far right until you get your desired contrast. Finally, to adjust the image's overall contrast, simply move the middle slider to the left or to the right to bring out more details.

Experimenting with Contrast

The Brightness tool is one that you will rarely use to edit images since it produces results that significantly change your image's overall appearance. However, for landscape photographs, it can be useful in editing image contrast if used sparingly.

To balance out the darkest areas of an image and its lightest parts, you can play around with the Brightness tool until you find the desired contrast. Moving the slider to the left side will lighten the darker portions of the image, while moving your slider to the right will increase the contrast levels of your image and cause a loss of detail.

To avoid making mistakes with the Brightness tool, attempt to utilize it mainly for black and white photographs. This way, you will be able to see the distinction between the dark and light areas with greater clarity.

Nevertheless, it is also possible to change a colored image into a grayscale one by playing with the Saturation tool at the right panel of the canvas. Move it to the left most part of the scale to remove all the color in the image. Another option is to select the Image menu, find Mode then select Grayscale.

Adjusting Hue and Saturation Levels

Playing with the Saturation tool requires some level of restraint. Increasing the saturation levels will likely bring out some colors that were not easily visible in the original image. Often, this could result in an overly contrasted image that has lost much of the original detail.

To avoid flattening your image, hone your skills on the more manageable editing tools before playing with the saturation. Often, you might even find yourself using the Saturation tool to tone down colors rather than to bring them out more. Less prominent color contrasts will create a more uniform and clean appearance on your photographs.

Spot Correcting

Sometimes, the image imperfections could also be the result of dirty camera lenses rather than careless photography. The fastest way to remove unwanted spots on your image is to use the Spot Healing Brush tool to blend them out. The tool comes in the shape of a Band-Aid and essentially performs the same function of providing speedy remedies to small problem areas.

With a few basic editing skills, you can easily correct minor imperfections and improve your photo's overall appearance. To find the best tips and tricks that will work for you, it is recommended that you experiment with the other editing tools until you find the settings that suit your taste. Play around with the levels until you find the right balance and avoid committing over-processing altogether.

Chapter 6 - Basics of the Pen Tool

Undoubtedly, Photoshop is best known as photo editing software. Nevertheless, it is also possible to use the program to create vector graphics. The easiest way to accomplish this more advanced skill is by using the Pen tool.

Manipulating the Pen tool is a skill that you can learn in a short amount of time. On the other hand, mastering the tool can take numerous practice sessions involving trial and error. Continuous practice will help you get a better grasp of the Pen tool's true potential.

What is the Pen tool?

Putting an actual pen to paper will allow you to create lines and shapes that will be limited only by your imagination. In essence, though, it will be unable to do little more than create marks on the surface.

With Photoshop's Pen tool, you will be able to create not only dots and dashes on your canvas. The powerful tool can immediately connect your dots in a certain way to create a freeform shape. This simple tool can help you draw vector graphics even with very little experience in graphic design applications.

Creating your Base Shapes

Though the Pen tool can appear deceptively simple and small, it can in fact perform the function of several tools. The fundamental way of using the tool involves clicking on your canvas to set up a few points. Lines will automatically join these points together as you go along. To create a straight line or perfect angle between points, simply hold down your shift key.

This basic function will result in freeform shapes that you can then manipulate to your desired form. However, if you need more precise forms and curved shapes, then you will need to tackle more advanced moves using the Pen tool.

Creating Curves

Similar to creating rough shapes, creating a curved form starts with setting up a single point on your canvas. After the first point, create another point without letting go of your mouse button. Continue to hold down your mouse and drag it to your desired spot. Instead of forming a straight line, a curved line will start to form between the points.

To create perfect angles every time, hold down the shift key as you drag. This move will also help you create more curves on your canvas. Instead of forming only a single line from one point to the next, you will end up with two lines coming out of a single point.

Each of those lines will have a small circle at the end. Dragging those circles around will adjust the specific line. One of the created lines will likely be touching the curved line. The line that is not touching the curved line will be the one to designate the next point you attempt to set.

To immediately apply changes to your new line, simply hold down the shift key on your PC or the options key on your Mac while dragging the curve into place. If you need to manipulate the curve after setting its position, then you can also hold down the shift or portion key then click on the end points of the curve to move it around.

It is important to note that longer lines will be harder to manipulate than shorter ones. The angles that they create will also have a greater effect on your succeeding curved lines. Sharper edges can be created using smaller angles, while rounder edges can be created from larger angles. The best way to understand the exact effect of the pen tool is to put it into practice and to start creating your own lines and shapes.

Using the Grid

If you still find it difficult to manipulate the Pen tool using only the abovementioned tips, another tool that can help facilitate the action is the Grid. The Grid is accessible from the Show submenu of the View menu window. The shortcut keys for the Grid are the ctrl key on a PC and command key on Mac.

Having a grid in place will help you better visualize the location of a point in space and allow you to plot your points more accurately. It can be particularly useful in crating symmetric shapes such as hearts or polygons.

Practice Makes Perfect

The Pen tool can be a tricky tool to master for many novice Photoshop users. For that reason, it is important to keep practicing with the tool to get a better grasp of its functions. One of the most enjoyable and easy ways to use the pen tool is to trace over actual photos instead of working from scratch. Go over the edges of your portraits to create a vector version of your face. Eventually, you will be able to move on to more complex projects once you master these basic tricks.

Conclusion

Thank you again for downloading this book!

I hope this book was able to help you learn more about Photoshop!

The next step is to put the strategies provided into use, and begin editing your photos with Photoshop!

Finally, if you enjoyed this book, please take the time to share your thoughts and post a review on Amazon. It'd be greatly appreciated!

Thank you and good luck!

www.ingramcontent.com/pod-product-compliance
Lightning Source LLC
Chambersburg PA
CBHW070906070326
40690CB00009B/2012